ACTING DOGS

BY MARIE PEARSON

Copyright © 2023 by Apex Editions, Mendota Heights, MN 55120. All rights reserved. No part of this book may be reproduced or utilized in any form or by any means without written permission from the publisher.

Apex is distributed by North Star Editions:
sales@northstareditions.com | 888-417-0195

Produced for Apex by Red Line Editorial.

Photographs ©: Shutterstock Images, cover, 1, 6, 7, 10–11, 13, 18–19, 20–21, 22–23, 24, 25, 26–27, 29; Lifestyle Pictures/Alamy, 4–5; George Rinhart/Corbis Historical/Getty Images, 8–9; A7A collection/Photo 12/Alamy, 15; iStockphoto, 16–17

Library of Congress Control Number: 2022912278

ISBN
978-1-63738-421-3 (hardcover)
978-1-63738-448-0 (paperback)
978-1-63738-501-2 (ebook pdf)
978-1-63738-475-6 (hosted ebook)

Printed in the United States of America
Mankato, MN
012023

NOTE TO PARENTS AND EDUCATORS

Apex books are designed to build literacy skills in striving readers. Exciting, high-interest content attracts and holds readers' attention. The text is carefully leveled to allow students to achieve success quickly. Additional features, such as bolded glossary words for difficult terms, help build comprehension.

TABLE OF CONTENTS

CHAPTER 1

A SCENE IN A FILM

I n the film *Togo*, a
puppy is in a barn.
He opens a cabinet door
with his paw. The puppy
goes into the cabinet.

Togo came out in 2019. It's about a sled dog who lived in the early 1900s.

BEHIND THE SCENES

In many  scenes, acting dogs look like they are doing things on their own. But trainers are there during the filming. They tell the dogs what to do.

Soon, he pops up through a hole in the countertop. The puppy jumps on an old shelf. He knocks jars to the floor.

Dogs practice skills with their trainers before filming.

Some dogs don't wear leashes when acting in movies. That way, they can move freely.

The puppy shoves a metal pipe away from a hole in the wall. He squeezes through the hole. He has escaped the barn!

FAST FACT

The movie *Togo* is based on a real dog. He was a Siberian husky.

The real Togo helped his owner win many dogsled races.

CHAPTER 2

AN ACTING DOG'S JOB

Acting dogs work in movies. They also appear in TV shows and **commercials**. Some dogs act in plays, too.

Like human actors, some dogs become very famous.

Some acting dogs belong to **professional** trainers. These dogs already know many commands. Trainers may teach dogs new tricks. Or trainers may buy or borrow dogs for certain projects.

FAST FACT

Many animals can learn to act. They include bears, monkeys, horses, and more.

Professional trainers often work with several different dogs. They teach each dog tricks.

Some people train their pet dogs to act. They can **audition** with a **talent agency**. This agency then helps the dogs find acting jobs.

A GROUP EFFORT

Sometimes, several dogs play the same character. One dog might be better at sitting calmly. Another might be better at barking or spinning. So, each dog acts in different scenes.

Four different dogs played the same character in the movie *Because of Winn-Dixie*.

CHAPTER 3

PERSONALITY

A film **set** is busy. It has many people, noises, and bright lights. Sometimes there are other animals. An acting dog can't be afraid.

A film set has many lights, sounds, and machines.

Acting dogs should also be friendly. Dogs often work with people and other animals, so they need to get along well. But dogs should also stay focused on their jobs.

Acting dogs need to be comfortable around other animals.

FAST FACT

Sometimes actors adopt the dogs they costar with.

Acting dogs need to be **obedient**. They don't always wear leashes on set. And they may be far from their trainer. So, dogs must listen carefully.

Acting dogs sometimes run through outdoor places.

STAYING SAFE

Many people work to keep animal actors safe. For example, the American Humane Association sends people to sets. They watch to make sure animals are treated well.

CHAPTER 4

TRICKS AND TRAINING

Acting dogs learn many skills and tricks. They practice staying, standing, sitting, and lying down.

Acting dogs go many places. Learning to stay is a key skill.

Acting dogs may need to pull or tug.

In some scenes, dogs bark or whine. They may hold things in their mouths. Or they may look in different directions. Sometimes, dogs have action scenes. They may run or leap over things.

TRAINING TRICKS

It's important that training is fun for dogs. Trainers use lots of treats. They also make training like a game. Dogs get treats for correct responses.

Treats help dogs learn which actions to do again.

Dogs in movies may look scared or angry. But trainers make sure they are safe and happy.

Dogs may also act in fight scenes. Usually, these dogs are just playing. Growling sounds are added later. Acting dogs should love their jobs!

FAST FACT

Some movies use computer-generated dogs for dangerous scenes. That way, real dogs stay safe.

COMPREHENSION QUESTIONS

Write your answers on a separate piece of paper.

1. Write a few sentences describing some tricks acting dogs might do.

2. Do you enjoy watching movies that have animal actors? Why or why not?

3. When dogs act in fight scenes, what are they usually doing?

    A. fighting

    B. staying

    C. playing

4. Why do acting dogs need to stay focused?

    A. so they can hear and obey their trainers

    B. so they can stay away from other people

    C. so they can bark louder

5. What does commands mean in this book?

These dogs already know many commands. Trainers may teach dogs new tricks.

    A. lists of rules people must follow

    B. ways of telling dogs what to do

    C. ways of keeping dogs from moving

6. What does dangerous mean in this book?

Some movies use computer-generated dogs for dangerous scenes. That way, real dogs stay safe.

    A. fun and easy

    B. safe and calm

    C. unsafe or risky

Answer key on page 32.

GLOSSARY

audition
To show skills as part of trying to get an acting job.

commercials
Short videos that try to get people to buy products.

computer-generated
Made with computers rather than real-life images.

obedient
Willing to do what one is told to do.

professional
Having to do with people who get paid for what they do.

scenes
The separate places and times shown in a movie, show, or play.

set
The place and objects used for a scene in a movie, show, or play.

talent agency
A company that helps other companies find and hire actors.

TO LEARN MORE

BOOKS

Marin, Vanessa Estrada. *Dog Training for Kids*. Penguin Random House, 2019.

Murray, Julie. *Acting Animals*. Minneapolis: Abdo Publishing, 2020.

Rich, Penelope. *Dog Tales: True Stories of Heroic Hounds*. London: Arcturus Publishing, 2021.

ONLINE RESOURCES

Visit www.apexeditions.com to find links and resources related to this title.

ABOUT THE AUTHOR

Marie Pearson is an author and editor of books for young readers. She has taught her standard poodle many tricks, including holding things in his mouth, spinning, and waving. He has auditioned with an animal talent agency.

INDEX

ANSWER KEY:
1. Answers will vary; 2. Answers will vary; 3. C; 4. A; 5. B; 6. C